Hercules Seghers

E. Haverkamp Begemann

Hercules Seghers

J. M. Meulenhoff Amsterdam 1968

Art and Architecture in the Netherlands

already published

J. B. Jongkind · John Raedecker · Neo-realism in painting · The "De Stijl" Group · The Experimentalists · Herman Kruyder · Van Dongen · Jaap Wagemaker · Henri ten Holt · Mari Andriessen · Kees Verwey · Jan Sluijters · Domela · Constant · André Volten · Geertgen tot Sint Jans · Gerrit Benner · Hendrik Chabot · Wessel Couzijn · Symbolism · Carel Visser · The Expressionists · J. J. P. Oud · K. P. C. de Bazel · L. C. van der Vlugt · B. Merkelbach

in preparation

G. H. Breitner · Corneille · Edgar Fernhout · Twentieth Century Dutch Graphic Art (I) · Isaac Israels · H. P. Berlage · Amsterdam School

A series of works on art and architecture in the Netherlands edited by:
R. Blijstra · D. Dooijes · J. Hulsker · H. L. C. Jaffé · Th. van Velzen · A. B. de Vries

Edward Norgate, the British miniaturist and art instructor of the sons of the second Earl of Arundel wrote in 1648–1650 in his *Miniatura or the Art of Limning* that landscape art was 'soe new in England, and soe lately come ashore, as all the Language within our fower Seas cannot find it a Name, but a borrowed one, and that from a people that are noe great Lenders but upon good Securitie, the Duch ... For to say truth the Art is theirs, and the best in that kind that ever I saw speake Dutch,...'. In these words he characterized very well the leading position of Netherlandish landscape artists in the beginning of the seventeenth century. As appears from his remarks following this quotation he was primarily thinking of Paulus Bril, Coninxloo, Porcellis, Vroom and Rubens, and therefore of two generations of Dutch and Flemish artists.

We now distinguish between that first generation of specialists, many of whom came from Antwerp, worked for some time in Frankenthal, then settled in Amsterdam, and the second generation mainly centered in Haarlem with Esaias van de Velde, Vroom, Buytewech, and Hercules Seghers. David Vinckboons, Gillis van Coninxloo and Joos de Momper belonged to the first generation; they all painted imaginary mountain landscapes and woods framing views of valleys or castles. They were pioneers in as much as they limited themselves to this one subject while creating at the same time a new style. For the members of the second generation this specialization came easily, but upon them fell the task to transform the inherited concepts. They chose two ways: one was to adopt the basic principles of the imaginary fantastic landscape and modify these, the other one was to throw these out completely and paint the countryside as they knew it. Various artists of this second generation did both, among them Hercules Seghers and Esaias van de Velde. The two had much in common: in 1612 at the age of about twenty-two they both entered the painters guild in Haarlem, therefore were both exposed to the tradition of Haarlem mannerism then still valid (Goltzius was 54 years old and still active), both were primarily interested in landscape, both etched as well as painted, and yet their roles in seventeenth-century Dutch art differed widely.

Already in 1614 Esaias started out by representing the Dutch countryside in a new revolutionary way, and developed this soon into a style which would set a trend for many decades to come. The naturalistic landscape in Dutch seventeenth-century art including one of its foremost representatives, Jan van Goyen, owes more to Esaias van de Velde than to anyone else. Occasionally Esaias van de Velde etched and painted imaginary mountainous landscapes, but he concentrated on the new trend of peaceful, quiet views of farms and rivers. Esaias van de Velde's break with the past consisted in creating a new type of landscape art.

Hercules Seghers, on the other hand, intensified the traditional imaginary mountain landscape and transformed it to such an extent that its origin was not recognizable any more. His hostile, barren valleys and mountains were so hauntingly inhuman that they created legends about his personality, and so thoroughly personal that he had no followers and little influence. Simultaneously with the imaginary mountain landscapes, at least during part of his incompletely established career, he made etchings of existing buildings such as the Abbey at Rijnsburg near Leiden, and of trees and woods he saw, and he etched and painted a few panoramic views of villages and of the town of Rhenen on the Rhine which seem a withdrawal from the visionary vistas of valleys of doom.

His Life: Facts and Legends

Before the works of Hercules Seghers are considered, the little that is known of his life should be mentioned. He probably was born in 1589 or 1590 in Haarlem since when he later settled in the Hague coming from Utrecht he was mentioned as 'Hercules of Haarlem'. He is known to have been a pupil of Gillis Coninxloo in Amsterdam until his teacher's death in December of 1606, and to have bought in March 1607 at the public sale of his master's estate one of his painting referred to as a 'Steenrootsken' and therefore probably representing rocks or a rocky landscape. This apprenticeship with Gillis van Coninxloo must have been of great significance for Hercules Seghers because it was probably in his studio and through him that he learned to know the mountain landscapes of some of his Flemish predecessors. Gillis van Coninxloo who had fled Antwerp for religious reasons and had settled in Amsterdam after having been some years at Frankenthal, may have introduced him to the works of Joos de Momper which made a great impression on him. Seghers' choice of a 'rocky landscape' in 1607 shows that already at the age of seventeen or eighteen the artist was fascinated by this subject. The painting must have been rather unusual for Gillis van Coninxloo, whose wooded landscapes in general do not seem to fit the title 'stony rock'. After Seghers had entered the guild in Haarlem in 1612, he is mentioned again in December of 1614 when he was engaged with Anneken van der Brugghen, a girl from Antwerp sixteen years his senior, to whom he was married in January of 1615. Eight days before the engagement Seghers arranged a settlement with Marritge Reyers, mother of his illegitimate daughter Nelletje Hercules. At that time the artist was living in Amsterdam and he therefore had not remained long in Haarlem after entering the guild. In 1619 Hercules Pietersz, as he then was called, bought a house on the Lindengracht from which he had a view on the Noorderkerk as he represented it in an etching (S. 49*, Fig. 15), and partly in the painting *Houses Overlooking a Valley* (Fig. 14). He lived in Amsterdam until 1631 when he moved to Utrecht where he stayed only briefly and where he is mentioned as selling certain paintings. He therefore was probably active as a dealer in works of art, a profession he exercised with two associates in 1633 in The Hague where he had settled in 1632. In the same city in 1638 a Cornelia de Witte is mentioned as the widow of Hercules Pietersz, and the conclusion is permissable that the artist had remarried and had died sometime betwee 1633 and 1638.

This is all that is known about Seghers' life. In addition, there are some early, partly contemporary references to his works. His fellow artists appreciated his paintings as we know from inventories of their belongings. In 1627 the Amsterdam painter Louys Rocourt had left two of Seghers' paintings in his estate, and the Rotterdam artist Herman Saftleven one; paintings by Seghers are also mentioned in 1639 in the estate of Anthony Gaillard and in 1649 in that of Jacob Marrell. Rembrandt owned in 1656 no less than eight paintings, among which probably the large *Mountain Valley* now in the Uffizi in Florence (Fig. 6 and 7). During his lifetime two of Seghers' paintings found their way into the collection of the House of Orange in the Hague in or before (1632) and one was offered for sale to the King of Denmark as early as 1621.

There cannot be any question therefore about the high esteem the artist received as a painter during his lifetime, and the story that he was not appreciated and died in greatest poverty as told by Samuel van Hoogstraten in 1678 needs to be reevaluated. Hoogstraten included in his 'biography' the following statement:

* S., followed by a number, refers to Jaro Springer's publication of Seghers' etchings (see *Bibliographical Note*, p. 25)

'Nobody wanted to look at his works during his lifetime: the printers took his prints by the basket to the merchants of butter and soap for them to wrap their wares and most of it ended up as paper bags. Finally he showed a plate as his masterpiece to an art dealer in Amsterdam and offered it for little money, but, imagine, the dealer complained that there was no market for his prints, and hardly thought it worthwhile to pay the cost of the copperplate so that poor Hercules had to return home disconsolate and after having printed a few copies from this plate he cut it into pieces, saying that the time would come that collectors would pay for one copy four times as much as he had asked for the whole plate, which actually did happen because each print later was paid sixteen ducats, and those who bought them praised themselves lucky for getting this chance; but poor Hercules did not get any of this, because although he used the linen of his shirts and beds for paintings and prints (because he also printed paintings), he remained in deepest poverty with his whole family. Finally his sorrowful wife complained that anything they had owned in the way of linen had been used for paintings or prints. This depressed Hercules so much, that being at wits end he wanted to drown his sorrows in wine, and returning home one evening more intoxicated than usual he fell off the stairs, and died; opening with his death the eyes of all art lovers who from that time on held his works in the high esteem they deserve and always will deserve.' Van Hoogstraten included this 'vita' in the chapter entitled 'how an artist should behave against the power of Fortune', and therefore used Seghers as an example of an artist who had lost the struggle against bad fortune. His death caused by drunkenness to which despair had brought him fits in the well known pattern of the artist endowed with genius and cursed by melancholy. He was one of the artists 'born under Saturn' and his life as told by Hoogstraten is reminiscent of that of Annibale Carracci and Adam Elsheimer told respectively by Baglione and Sandrart.

Hoogstraten's relative neglect of the artist's activity as a painter may be a clue to a better understanding of his description of the life of the artist. He started out by saying that Seghers was a good landscape artist and that he seemed 'pregnant of whole Provinces to which he gave life with immense spaces in his Paintings and Prints" (the similarity to Van Mander's statement that Pieter Bruegel was said to have swallowed up the Alps and regurgitated them on panels and canvases upon his return home may not be accidental), but did not say anything more about this aspect of the artist's activity which according to the sources was so successful. Hoogstraten had a good first hand knowledge of Seghers' prints, because he knew that Seghers 'printed' paintings, sometimes on linen, that he cut plates, and that he pulled very few impressions only, and we may therefore assume that his story of the lack of success of Seghers as a printmaker was primarily based on his knowledge of the prints rather than of the factual circumstances. Not understanding fully the very nature of these prints of which each single one was an experiment he misinterpreted the small number of impressions pulled and applied the apparent lack of success to all his work. Whether Seghers actually was poor is not known. The references to his debts in contemporary documents should not necessarily give the impression of poverty, since borrowing money then was as usual as it is nowadays and because the majority of documents about seventeenth century artists concern debts and borrowings (without these we would know as little about these artists as about the painters of the fifteenth century). That Seghers dealt in works of art is not a sign of poverty either: dealing was not unusual as a side occupation for artists in the Netherlands in the seventeenth century.

His Work: Mountain Landscapes

The eleven paintings that can be considered without any doubt as having been made by him represent exclusively landscapes, and those that are mentioned in early records and inventories and which are lost were all landscapes with one or two exceptions, the more than life-size painting of a skull and perhaps a 'Virgin and Child'. The great majority of the etchings also represent landscapes, and therefore the paintings and etchings of landscapes will be discussed first.

Seghers' etched landscapes range between two extremes: on the one hand the fantastic, imaginary views of deserted valleys surrounded by wild rock formations, on the other side the naturalistic views of fields with distant villages. The printed landscapes of the first group predominate in numbers while there are only two properly speaking panoramic views of Dutch villages (S. 34 and S. 35, Fig. 21c) of which in total five impressions exist. In between these extremes there is in the prints a whole scale of variations: there are the ruins of the Abbey at Rijnsburg, represented rather faithfully but in one print in mood transposed into a different world (S. 53 and S. 54, Figs. 16 and 17), and the highly fantastic mountain land-scape where one suddenly discovers, far in the distance, a village known from one of the paintings of Dutch panorama landscapes (S. 14, with houses and a church tower similar to those of the painting in Berlin). In the painted land-scapes the range from fantastic to naturalistic is also fully represented. Although the chronology of Seghers' work is far from clear it is likely that the painted moun-tain landscapes belong to the early part of his career and that the views of villages were painted later. The paintings and the etchings will be discussed in that order (although some etchings of mountains seem late and of Dutch scenery early).

Two paintings, very much alike in scenery, composition, and color, and both signed may have been done before 1620, the *River Valley* in the Rijksmuseum in Amsterdam (Fig. 4) and the *Mountain Valley* in the collection of Mrs. E. Kessler-Stoop in IJmuiden (to the same group belonged a painting now lost but known through a drawing after it by L. Bramer). In the Amsterdam painting a wide valley stretches far towards the horizon and is closed in the far distance and at the sides by greenish grey mountains, shaped as meaningless clumps. The foreground is marked by hills with broken tree trunks, a solitary traveler at the left, and two forlorn people at the right. In composition the painting is similar to one of the few imaginary valleys that Seghers printed in black only, the *Winding River in a Valley* (S. 24, Fig. 1; another impression of the plate is printed in black on dark violet colored paper). In this beautiful, spacious landscape, more extensively cultivated and more inhabitable than any of his mountain landscapes, a meander-ing river flows through a valley seen behind rocky cliffs with a log cabin and some other dwellings in the foreground. The width of the river and vastness of the valley itself are indicated by the trees in the distance and especially by the tiny sail boats on the water.

A number of etchings such as *The Enclosed Valley* (S. 12, Figs. cover, 2 and 3) and *Rocky Landscape with a Plateau* (S. 17, Fig. III), where plateaus are sur-rounded by mountains, or the *Rocky River Landscape with a Road* (S. 25) which in the shapes of the rocks is closer to the moon landscape as we now know it than any other print of the seventeenth century, represent hauntingly inhuman landscapes similar to those of the Amsterdam painting and the related one in the Kessler Collection. The shadows are menacing, the crevices in the rocks seem pitfalls for any man who would dare to enter these deserts of rock and stone. To the same group of rocky mountain landscapes belongs the *Mountain Landscape with Rigging of a Ship* (S. 7, Fig. 8) where a road with wheel tracks winds itself over cliffs to a windmill precariously perched on a hill farther down. Beyond the mill, deep down between the mountains in shadows which seem eternal, lies a village with a church. The desolateness of the scene is intensified by the three tree stumps in the foreground and the minute traveler who emerges from behind the foreground hill. The same elements, stumps of broken trees, a road, a lonely village, and rock formations are found in other etchings, such as the *Landscape with a Man Carrying a Stick* (S. 16) or the *Landscape with a Waterfall* (S. 21, Fig. 9). Very close to the painting in the Kessler Collection, even repeating its composition in reverse and probably made after it, is the large etching *Mountain Valley with Four Trees* (S. 28, Fig. 5). Only after observing the print for some time one realizes that in the distance a few houses are clustered together amidst trees which only intensify the desolation and increase the size of the towering rocks at the left.

This large print – the largest impression measures 28.7×47.1 cm. – belongs to a group of three very large etchings. The other two are the *Large Rocky Landscape with Waterfalls* (S. 30) which is closely related to the two paintings, and the *Landscape with Fenced Fields* (S. 29, Fig. 11) which has a somewhat more peaceful and inviting nature. The fields separated from each other by hedges and fences, the farms, and the large city in the distance give this print a human element which contrasts with the awesome rocks at the left and the mountains at the right. One impression of this print (Dresden) is no less than 52.2 cm., the one here reproduced (Fig. 11) is 49.2 cm. wide. Such large formats were not used for landscapes in the first half of the seventeenth century except for profiles or birds-eye views of cities which had an official or representative character. It is one instance of Seghers' efforts to approximate in prints the effects of paintings, of which more instances will be discussed later.

Since the known paintings do not follow one another in a sequence showing in each case consequential changes in Seghers' style, and since the prints are hardly of any help in this respect, an absolute chronology of Seghers' work cannot be established at this point. It also is not known how many paintings are lost, and whether those preserved are representative of all phases of his development. It only may be surmised that of the known paintings the small *River Landscape with a Waterfall* at Castle Herdringen in Westphalia followed the Amsterdam and Kessler paintings after a relatively short interval (it probably is identical with a painting mentioned in an inventory of 1627). It is similar to those in the thin application of paint, in the manner of painting, and in the color scheme based on greys and greens with only a few brighter notes in the red roof of a house, and a touch of blue and orange in the sky.

Probably some time after the two mountain landscapes just discussed Seghers painted the landscape that undoubtedly is his most accomplished, most impressive, and largest painting, namely the *Mountain Valley* in the Uffizi in Florence (Figs. 6 and 7). The heavy rock formations at the right contrast with the flat meadows and fields, bordered by trees in the distance, painted with heavier paint and in greater detail. A barren landscape in the foreground and some pine trees which are partly dead partly alive serve as an introduction to the vast view into the distance. This expanse of fertile land seems tantalizingly inviting beyond the barren foreground, but the menacing rocks warn against an optimistic anticipation of nature's blessings. These tensions are increased by the light of a threatening storm while heavy clouds intercept part of the sunlight. The colors are predominantly shades of browns and greens, with touches of yellow and red, and other colors mainly in the distant vista.

This landscape, bequeathed to the Uffizi in 1838 as a work of Rembrandt, was the first painting to be recognized as a work of Seghers. In 1871 Wilhelm von Bode and Baron von Liphart independently attributed it to him on the basis of its similarity with some of his etchings. Paradoxically it now generally is assumed that Rembrandt not only owned the painting but also repainted it. The painting must be identical with the one landscape distinguished as 'large' among the eight by Seghers that Rembrandt owned in 1656 when it was listed as hanging in the large rear room 'agtercamer offte sael.' At the left Rembrandt added the wagon pulled by two horses and driven by one man while another is walking at the side. With these figures actively engaged in their rural duties Rembrandt introduced a human element purposefully omitted by Seghers who never included figures of such human countenance. Rembrandt most likely also overpainted some of the mountains at the right and part of the sky, thus increasing the sense of drama on one side while adding a human touch on the other. His changes are particularly clear in the mountains in the distance at the right where his heavy *impastos* contrast with the thinly applied brushstrokes showing much of the panel between them in the rocks at the lower right. The massive rocks, strongly lit by the sun, and the dark high range behind them were painted almost entirely by Rembrandt over darker mountains which in Seghers' version also had a different, more rounded and less jagged silhouette. Rembrandt probably also re- touched sections of the middle foreground. As Wolfgang Stechow wrote, Rem- brandt made a second state of the painting as he did with Seghers' etching of *Tobias and the Angel*.

The basic structure of the painting remains a work of Seghers, and large areas were not touched by Rembrandt such as the lightly and thinly painted areas in the rocks at the right. In tone and execution these are reminiscent of the Amster- dam and Kessler paintings. In this respect, and also in their shape, these rocks are very similar to details of Joos de Momper's rocky landscapes, and to some extent they must be based on his work. The idea, however, of combining such rocks with flat land and of intensifying the resulting contrast, which is the essence of this painting, is personal and new. Once Seghers had given expression to this idea, he used it repeatedly in paintings as well as in etchings, varying the formula and stressing sometimes the atmosphere of tension where mountains are wild and high, or emphasizing a more gentle aspect of nature where the pastures and fields prevail and the hills take the place of the mountains. Closest in mood to the Uffizi painting are among the etchings the *Landscape with Fenced Fields* (S. 29, Fig. 11) and the *Landscape with the Branch of a Pine Tree* (S. 11, Plates I and II). In both we find the combination of threatening rocks and peaceful flat land, of the exotic and the autochthonous, of rivers and dwellings. Other etchings that are basically representations of the same combination of distant views and moun- tains are farther removed from the Uffizi paintings. Some of these will be discussed later.

In addition to the Uffizi *Mountain Valley* there are no less than three paintings which combine such distant views and mountains (two in Rotterdam, and one in the Historical Society in New York). Probably shortly after the Uffizi landscape Seghers painted *The Valley* and the *Houses Overlooking a Valley*, both in the Boymans-van Beuningen Museum in Rotterdam (Figs. 10, 12 and 14). *The Valley* is painted on canvas stretched over panel as is the Uffizi landscape, a combination of 'carriers' occasionally used by other artists but apparently particularly liked by Seghers. In comparison with the Uffizi painting, the mountains at the right in *The Valley* are reduced to hills covered with trees and bushes with a type of foliage consisting of groups of dots and circles, characteristic for a number of Seghers' paintings and prints. The tower and round building in the middle distance beyond an island embedded in a river are reminiscent of other similar buildings in some of Seghers' prints, especially in *The Large Tree* (S. 39, Fig. 19), and in their isolation in the landscape and the separation from each other they look like a displaced *baptisterium* with a free standing *campanile*. In the far distance is a vast lake with sailboats. In its composition this painting is similar, in reverse, to that of the etching *The Oak* (S. 40, Fig. 18), printed in black on white prepared linen. The distant landscape with sailboats on a lake, the tower and the circular building, the hills on one side and the elevated foreground with a road are all present in both the painting and the etching, which therefore may have originated approximately at the same time, around 1620–1627.

The painting *Houses Overlooking a Valley* (Fig. 14), formerly in the D. G. van Beuningen Collection and since 1958 in the Museum in Rotterdam, is a particularly fascinating example of familiar scenery in an imaginary setting. Formerly this painting was called 'The Meuse Valley' because of a general similarity between the site represented and certain stretches of the valley of that river South of Liège where the rocky mountains are close to the river bordered by wide, flat expanses. It is possible that the artist incorporated in this painting reminiscenses of a trip to the Meuse Valley, but it certainly is not an exact representation of it. The group of houses in the foreground are those which Seghers saw from the window of his house on the Lindengracht in Amsterdam. We know these houses from the detailed map of the city made by Balthasar Florisz in 1625, and also from Seghers' own etching representing the opened window itself with the houses as seen through it (S. 49, Fig. 15). Including the frame of a window was a novelty, at least it is very likely that the etching preceded the *Stormy Sea* painted in 1629 by Jan Porcellis (Munich, Bayerische Staatsgemäldesammlungen) where the window frame is included, and it certainly preceded Herman Saftleven's view of houses in Utrecht seen through a window (drawing in Amsterdam). Apart from some liberties taken by the artist in the distance at the right where a glimpse of the center of Amsterdam would have been more appropriate than trees, the etching provides a rather faithful representation of that part of the city. Seghers simplified the church representing as a flat wall what actually is a combination of a wall and a receding roof, by omitting the traceries of the windows and by omitting other details (other architectural features make it likely that some secondary structures had not yet been finished at the time). The houses in the foreground, however, are represented as they were, and most of them are found in the painting only with such minor changes as one or two added façades making the silhouette against the landscape more interesting. Seghers thus transposed these houses into new surroundings, and in order to obtain a smooth transition between the hilly landscape in the foreground and the houses he transformed the wooden fence hiding the lower parts of the house from view into a dark earthen wall covered with plants without, however, defining it clearly.

It is no exception in Dutch seventeenth century art that existing buildings were put in imaginary landscapes. Salomon van Ruysdael and others placed the Pellekussenpoort located near Utrecht into imagined river landscapes; St. Mary's Church was transplanted by Jan van Goyen, Albert Cuyp and others from the center of Utrecht into hilly landscapes. This practice is already found in a drawing by Jacques de Gheyn (1565–1629) where the Amsterdam tower 'Swijght-Utrecht' in somewhat modified form is found in a wild mountain landscape. These other displaced monuments are well known buildings, but it is very well possible that other artists when they wanted to paint houses represented those most readily available, although no other examples have been identified.

Seghers's new idea of combining a wide view of flat land beyond a foreground of hills or houses with mountains or hills at one side is also found in a painting which unfortunately has suffered from neglect and damage, and which only recently has been recognized as a work of Hercules Seghers. This painting, *Houses and a Village in a River Valley*, in the New York Historical Society, also shows the trees and bushes familiar from the two Rotterdam paintings, and even the wide lake at the horizon with some tiny sailboats.

His Work: Trees, Ruins and Villages

Although *The Large Tree* (S. 39. Fig. 19), one of Seghers' most admired etchings, has much in common with the three paintings just discussed in such details as the background, the buildings and the foliage, the main theme and the total effect are completely different. The subject is a large, strong and broad but not very tall, old and still very healthy tree growing on a grassy bank. Standing in the middle foreground it attracts all the attention which is focused on it by the composition of the print. The massiveness of the tree is stressed by the format of the print which is considerably wider than high, and by its contrasting with the small buildings and trees at its sides. In seventeenth-century art of the Netherlands the tree was a subject by itself, and many artists have made paintings, drawings and etchings with a single tree as the main subject. Hendrick Goltzius, Adam Elsheimer, Jan van Goyen and Jacob Ruisdael should be mentioned as the most distinguished ones, but not one of their trees is as imposing, as massive, as firmly rooted as this one. Not only is the tree heavy, it has a threatening, obsessing quality, mainly produced by the repetition of contrasts of countless white and black dots, dashes and lines. If one is asked to identify the tree, the answer is difficult to give. It could be an oak, but Seghers obviously was more interested in producing his image of a tree than in faithfully representing a particular one.

The same is true of the etching *Two Trees* (S. 38, Fig. 24), printed in brown on paper colored blue, rose and a little green and yellow. The trees, not rooted in any soil and placed against no other background than the colored paper, mysteriously evoke Far Eastern art. They are the most delicate and poetic trees Seghers ever made, although not the most mysterious and exotic ones. The *Mossy Tree* (S. 37, Fig. IV) has no trunk, no body, only weird branches covered with a growth that looks like Spanish moss or sea weed. This airy *Mossy Tree* and the delicate *Two Trees* contrast sharply with the heavy *Large Tree*, and show of what a range of expressions the artist is capable. Even greater is the distance between these trees and the desolate mountain landscapes. If it would be possible to reconstruct the personality of an artist from his works of art only, it would seem as if in this case two distinct personalities were involved.

Equally distant from the mountain landscapes are the paintings and prints of cities and villages. The painted *View of Brussels* (Cologne, Wallraf-Richartz-Museum; Fig. 20) has no fantastic rocks, nor broken trees, and shows the city faithfully depicted from the North as comparison with an earlier drawing by Hans Bol and later representations by Philippe de Champaigne and others show. With the *View of Rhenen* in the Museum in Berlin (Fig. 21 center) it is Seghers' most naturalistic painting. Seghers painted other views of cities which are lost (a *View of the Noorderkerk in Amsterdam*, and a painting of *Houses* are only known from inventories) and his activity as a painter of cities and buildings therefore must have been more intense than the few examples that survived seem to indicate.

An existing building is also represented in the two etchings of *The Abbey at Rijnsburg* (S. 53 and 54, Figs. 16 and 17). The large hall of the Benedictine Abbey near Leiden probably was destroyed in 1573/74 when the Spaniards tried to capture Leiden, but the remains were still standing in the seventeenth century. Of the two etchings, the smaller (S. 53, Fig. 16), in style close to *The Oak* (S. 40, Fig. 18) and always printed on linen, is more a factual and objective representation of the abbey than the larger one (S. 54, Fig. 17) which through the heavier contrasts and the colors Seghers used has become an expression of transitoriness rather than a depiction of a building. By printing some impressions of this *Large Ruin of the Abbey at Rijnsburg* in white or yellowish green on paper colored black, Seghers obtained a phosphorescent night effect. His contemporaries (Jan and Esaias van de Velde, Willem Buytewech, and others) often represented ruins, partly for what we would call their 'picturesque' qualities, and partly as signs of the greatness of the national past and of the transitoriness of all that man makes, but not one of them has endowed them with a similar mood of stagnation of life and inevitable decay.

Of the naturalistic paintings and prints the views of Rhenen and of two unidentified villages are the most advanced if compared with contemporary landscapes by Jan van de Velde, Jan van Goyen and others. They are panoramic landscapes with a rather high horizon, and a village or city situated just beyond the middle ground. The *View of Rhenen* (Fig. 21 center) wich was signed by Seghers, but which was provided with a signature of Van Goyen when it entered the Berlin Museum, was probably painted before 1630/31 because a palace then constructed seems to be absent, but how long before that date is not known (unfortunately the painting is not in a very good condition). The other two, the *Village on a River*, also in the Museum in Berlin (Fig. 21 top), and *The Two Windmills* in the Collection of Mrs. E. S. Borthwick Norton, Fareham, England, probably preceded the first one. As J. G. van Gelder recognized, all three paintings were changed in the seventeenth century by the addition of a sky. These additions undoubtedly were added in order to 'modernize' the paintings and to bring them up to date with those made by Jan van Goyen and others around 1640, and it is very well possible that these skies were added on behalf of the art dealer Johannes de Renialme who owned so many of Seghers' paintings. A fact is that the additions to the *Village on a River* in Berlin and *The Two Windmills* in Mrs. Borthwick Norton's collection were painted by the same artist. The *Village on a River* in Berlin is now framed in such a way that the added sky is concealed under the frame.

Seghers etched two panoramic views (S. 34 and 35) which are closely connected with *The Two Windmills* and the *View of Rhenen*. One etching (S. 35, Fig. 21 bottom) representing in reverse the same site as the former painting with mountains added in the distance probably was made after that painting. The second etching (S. 34) is another view of Rhenen. It is not clear, however, whether the etching followed the painting or vice versa, neither to what extent painting and etching are faithful renderings of the town. Although there is no certainty about their time of origin it is tempting to consider these Dutch views as representing Seghers' last stage in landscape art. It remains possible that Seghers painted and etched some of these Dutch landscapes simultaneously with the imaginary mountain valleys. In any event, if the *View of Rhenen* was painted before 1630/ 1631, Seghers then would have preceded, at least in paintings, Jan van Goyen, who used the same format for the same type of landscape in the early 1630's.

His Work: Other Subjects

Apart from landscapes, Seghers painted only few other subjects none of which has been preserved. It is known that in addition to houses and a view of the Noorderkerk which are somewhat related to landscapes, Seghers also made a more than life-size painting of a skull (67×86 cm.), which in 1663 was presented to the Surgeons Guild in Amsterdam and which unfortunately is lost out of sight since 1853. In 1663 it was reported to have been painted after a skeleton of someone 'from a very distant country', which had been sent to the King of France and which was shown in The Netherlands by an itinerant nobleman. It therefore probably was the skull of a native of a non European country, or at least it was shown as such, and caught the attention of Seghers. It may have been the same skull Seghers represented in the small etching (S. 61) known only in one impression in the Rijksmuseum in Amsterdam. The subject of a skull certainly agrees very well in mood with the few desolate, gloomy rocky landscapes Seghers painted and the larger number he etched.

Seghers expressed the same sentiments in two etchings of storms at sea. One represents a small sailboat tossed by high waves (S. 58), the other one (S. 59, Fig. 22) three sailboats battling the elements, while a huge whale swims spouting in the foreground where also a bale of goods is floating on the waves. The subject is that of the famous painting in Vienna alternatively attributed to Pieter Bruegel the Elder and Joos de Momper: an object is tossed to the whale in an effort to detract him from the ship. Whether it is successful in Seghers' etching is doubtful, since one of the three ships is sinking. The sea is boiling, the sky is equally turbulent, and since the etching is printed in green on paper first covered with a layer of black oil paint the impression is that of utter desolation. Nowhere in seventeenth century art are the forces of nature and man's helplessness in countering them expressed so dramatically.

Of other etchings only the remarkable *Three Books* (S. 62, Fig. 23) should be mentioned. Until Wenzel Hollar decided that muffs were a proper subject for a print, still life was limited to painting. Seghers' still life of books is one of the very few of such prints, but it is more. The books are not displayed on a course wooden surface, they are lying as if they have been left by someone who was reading them, one large folio open on top of another one, and as if to mark a page a smaller, perhaps octavo volume, is left in between its pages. Because of this arrangement, and perhaps because of the somber colors (printed in green and colored with grey-black or brown-black), the print is related in sentiment and meaning to Bruegel's drawing *Big Fish Eat Little Fish* (Vienna).

Technique

In the previous brief discussion of Seghers' works a few remarks have been made about some of the technical aspects of his prints. The technique of Seghers' prints poses problems which have not yet been solved. All the prints have the character of experiments. Seghers had no publisher — Hoogstraten knew that — and probably did not want one — which Hoogstraten did not understand. He never pulled many impressions: about 183 impressions are known of approximately 54 plates, which is a little over three impressions to the plate. No two impressions are the same.

Seghers sometimes is unduely credited with the invention of color printing. He did use green, yellow, blue, and white ink instead of black, but he never printed with more than one color in one print and never used more than one plate for a print. He printed on linen as well as on paper, and covered both often with color (generally water color or body color) before printing on it, and often used for printing ink of a different shade of the same color he had used for preparing the ground (printing in dark blue on light blue, etc.). Afterwards Seghers often touched the impressions or repainted them extensively, and also made counterproofs, on paper as well as on linen, and repainted these. One other peculiar characteristic of Seghers' prints is the way he cut them on all sides. We must assume that the artist as nowadays photographers cropped his prints in various ways in order to obtain different compositions.

This is not the place to discuss in detail Seghers' use of mordants, tools and grounds, and, in general, his etching technique. Many art historians and artists have tried to unravel the 'mysterious' aspects of Seghers' etching technique, without reaching a definitive conclusion. It seems that in these discussions too much importance has been attached to technical, and not enough to stylistic matters. Most of the effects of his etchings Seghers could have obtained with regular etching, the use of stop-out varnish, dry-point, and by wiping certain areas of a plate less strongly than others. In some instances he must have covered most of the copper plate with a dense network of cross hatching, and then etched this into the plate. *The Large Tree* (Fig. 19) for instance shows clearly this all over pattern. Here it is combined with white dots, which probably were obtained with the brush and stop-out varnish, and with flowing, flexible black lines which must have been produced by etching or in a technique generally known as sugar bite or lift ground technique. It at least is very likely that Seghers used this technique in another print, the *Winding River in a Valley* (Fig. 1). This technique was only rarely used until Chagall, Picasso and contemporaries revived it about fifty years ago. In the case of the *Winding River in a Valley* Seghers probably sketched with a brush on the copper plate.

Since it is not possible to discuss further details of Seghers' variations in printing and inking, a few specific examples may be mentioned. The two impressions of

The Enclosed Valley here reproduced (Figs. cover, 2 and 3) show only some of these variations. Seghers printed the impression in the Rijksmuseum in Amsterdam (Fig. 2) in blue on white paper, subsequently colored it with a brush and greyish green and purplish watercolor, and then applied to the sky and the mountains in the distance a very thin layer of a whitish haze, thus increasing the impression of distance. He washed the mountains in the foreground and the middle distance in such a way that at the left a large vertical rock formation stands out in front of mountains farther back. The London impression (Fig. cover and 3) is quite different. After having printed the image in black on linen which he previously had colored light brown, Seghers colored the print in blue (background), brown (foreground) and grey. By coloring the mountains differently Seghers fused the mountains at the left into one solid mass thus creating a different spatial effect. By using different colors and applying them in different areas Seghers could vary endlessly the total aspect of this print of which more impressions exist than of any other plate of his (about 21). He printed this particular plate in blue, green, or black on paper or linen colored yellow, grey, green, brown or blue of various shades and intensities, and then colored the print in various colors. The two impressions here reproduced are both without shadowing obtained with light hatching in drypoint which Seghers added in a second state. There exists also a counterproof on linen, heavily covered with watercolor (Dresden).

These prints therefore have many characteristics of paintings. Hoogstraten's statement that Seghers 'printed paintings' is therefore entirely correct, and equally appropriately has his wish to print paintings been called his 'obsession'. One of his prints that comes closest to a painting is the *Landscape with Branch of a Pine Tree* in Amsterdam (S. 11, Plate II) which is the only counterproof of a composition of which seventeen impressions exist. The impression here reproduced for comparison, also in the Rijksmuseum (Plate I), is printed in dark brown ink on light reddish prepared paper. The counterproof on the other hand is obtained from a dark green impression and printed on linen previously colored with very light brown watercolor, and subsequently overpainted with yellow-green oilpaint and with a little light rose at the horizon. The print is so similar to an oil sketch that it was classified as such by Springer in his basic study of Seghers' etchings. Other impressions of the same plate are in green on prepared paper, or in blue, white or yellow on light blue prepared or even in blue on yellow prepared paper, and afterwards many of the impressions were touched up in a variety of colors.

Sometimes Seghers varnished the print entirely or partly, thus approximating the effect of painting even closer. One impression of the *Large Ruin of the Abbey at Rijnsburg* is printed in yellow on black painted paper, then colored green for the sky and red for the bricks, and finally varnished. The etching *The Two Windmills* (Fig. 21 bottom) is printed in very dark green on green prepared paper, then extensively 'colored' (the houses red, the water blue, the roads yellow, the mountains brown and yellow, the sky blue and red). Finally only the houses were varnished.

Originality; Influence

Was Seghers without any precedent? In many respects his work and his methods are reminiscent of earlier artistic and technical achievements. His concept of the mountain landscape owes much to that of Joos de Momper, and also to chiaroscuro woodcuts of Hendrick Goltzius, his representations of trees and hills to Adam Elsheimer – one of whose compositions of *Tobias and the Angel* he copied in an etching – and he probably also knew and admired the landscapes of early sixteenth century German artists such as Altdorfer (he copied Baldung Grien's woodcut of the Lamentation). Technically, printing on cloth was not a novelty, neither was touching up impressions. Woodcuts on linen were not uncommon in the fifteenth century, and Andrea Andreani, to mention one example close to Seghers in time, printed his *Triumph of Caesar* after Andrea Mantegna in 1599 in black on black satin and added the highlights with a very fine brush in gold, while Hendrick Goudt printed at least one of his prints after Adam Elsheimer's *Tobias and the Angel* (1608) on silk. Whether lift ground was used before it was applied by Seghers needs to be investigated.

Seghers did, however, more than transform existing styles into a personal idiom and traditional motifs into personal imaginations. He created a type of landscape unknown to Dutch seventeenth-century art: the combination of 'Dutch' flat landscape with 'foreign', imaginary mountains or hills, mainly on one side of the composition. As for the graphic techniques, he probably did not invent any one of them, but unprecedented was his search for a combination of these techniques which would surpass the limits of each of them.

Remains the question of his impact on contemporaries and later generations. This is difficult to assess as far as the members of his own generation are concerned because of the lack of securely dated paintings and etchings. It is for instance not clear whether Cornelis Vroom (1590/91–1681) whose drawings of polders and lakes beyond dunes sometimes are related to Seghers' paintings of the type of *The Valley* (Rotterdam) or the etching *The Oak* (S. 40), was stimulated by Seghers or whether they both came independently to the same solutions for similar problems. It is certain, however, that only one artist of his generation (if he still belongs to it: he was about thirteen years younger) followed him in some respects so closely that his paintings almost look like imitations of paintings of the type of the Amsterdam painting. This artist was Frans de Momper, born in 1603, who probably learned to appreciate Seghers' paintings at the Hague or Amsterdam where he worked for some time.

Of the younger artists Rembrandt was by far the most strongly impressed by Seghers' paintings, particularly by his wild mountain landscapes. When he painted his own imaginary landscapes, especially the *Stormy Lamdscape with the Good Samaritan* (1638), now in Cracow, and the *Stormy Landscape* in Braunschweig, he clearly showed his admiration for the older artist and introduced a similar mood and atmosphere. In one painting, *The Landscape with a Drawbridge* in the Collection of the Duke of Berwick and Alba in Madrid, there seem to be reminiscencies in some details of landscapes of the type of the Uffizi *Mountain Valley* or the Rotterdam *Valley*. As has been mentioned already, Rembrandt owned the Uffizi *Mountain Valley* and seven other paintings by or attributed to Seghers, and he also owned and reworked the plate of Seghers' etching *Tobias and the Angel* (after a composition of Elsheimer) into a *Flight into Egypt*.

It is also perhaps through Rembrandt's collection of Seghers' paintings or due to his admiration of the artist that one of his pupils, Philips Koninck (1619–1688) was influenced by another aspect of Seghers' landscapes, namely the combination of flat land and rhythmically arranged fields and meadows with high hills in the foreground as we find them in the Rotterdam *Valley* and the Uffizi *Mountain Valley*. Especially some of his drawings are in composition directly related to Seghers' paintings.

Few traces of Seghers' painted landscapes are found in the works of other artists. Jan van Goyen and Pieter Molijn, born respectively 1596 and 1595, Aert van der Neer (born *c.* 1603), Herman Saftleven (born 1609) and Albert Cuyp (born 1620) show knowledge of the same features of Seghers' paintings that interested Philips Koninck, but these instances are few.

The only seventeenth-century graphic artist who was influenced by Seghers' etchings was Johannes Ruyscher who in his landscape drawings could not escape the powerful impact of Rembrandt's drawings. He must have had first hand knowledge of the etchings, may even have owned some.

Ruyscher, however, was primarily taken by Seghers' etchings of Dutch Villages and of Rhenen, and of the distant vistas in the mountain landscapes, rather than by the rocks and mountains themselves. Contemporaries knew of the relation between his work and that of Seghers and named him 'the young Hercules'.

Besides Johannes Ruyscher not one other seventeenth-century artist was influenced by Seghers' etchings, and even he was hardly stirred by the fantastic mountain views, and did not try to emulate his technical experiments. Seghers' concept of an imaginary, dehumanized world was too far outside the development of any trend of landscape art in the Netherlands to be adopted by other artists.

Hamden, Connecticut, August 1966

Bibliographical note

The sources and data of Seghers' life, and a comprehensive yet concise discussion of the paintings and of many aspects of the etchings, as well as a complete bibliography until 1936 are found in the exemplary article by Eduard Trautscholdt, *s.v.* Seghers, in Thieme-Becker, *Allgemeines Lexikon der bildenden Künstler*, XXX, Leipzig 1936, pp. 444–458. The best article on his paintings since then was also written by Dr. Trautscholdt and appeared under the title 'Neues Bemühen um Hercules Seghers' in *Imprimatur*, XII, 1954/55, pp. 78–85. The best general introduction to his art are Wilhelm von Bode's essay in *Rembrandt und seine Zeitgenossen*, Leipzig 1906, based on his earlier article of 1903 in the *Jahrbuch der preussischen Kunstsammlungen* and most recently reprinted in his *Die Meister der holländischen und flämischen Malerschulen*, ed. E. Plietzsch, Leipzig 1951, and the sections on Seghers in the excellent recent book by Wolfgang Stechow, *Dutch Landscape Painting of the Seventeenth Century*, London 1966. The monograph by Leo C. Collins, *Hercules Seghers*, Chicago 1953, is full of errors.
The basic publication on the etchings is the facsimile edition of Jaro Springer, *Die Radierungen des Herkules Seghers*, three volumes with 66 plates, catalogue volume, and separate introduction, Berlin 1910–1912 (Graphische Gesellschaft, fascicules XIII, XIV and XVI, and unnumbered 'Verzeichnis'). The technique of Seghers' etchings has recently been discussed in a book by Willem van Leusden, *Het grafisch-technisch probleem van de etsen van Hercules Seghers*, Utrecht 1960 (translated under the title *The Etchings of Hercules Seghers and the Problems of his Graphic Technique*, Utrecht, 1961) and in an article by Jacques Houplain, 'Sur les estampes d'Hercules Seghers', in *Gazette des Beaux-Arts*, VIe période, tome 49, 1957, pp. 149–164; neither is fully satisfactory. Recent valuable contributions on Seghers' etchings were written by J. Q. van Regteren Altena, 'Hercules Seghers en de topographie', in *Bulletin van het Rijksmuseum*, III, 1955, pp. 3–8, and K. G. Boon, 'Een notitie op een Seghers-prent uit de verzameling Hinloopen' in the same *Bulletin*, VIII, 1960, pp. 3–11.
The quotation from Edward Norgate's *Miniatura or the Art of Limning* is taken from the edition of Martin Hardie, Oxford 1919, p. 42; that from Samuel van Hoogstraten's *Inleyding tot de Hooge Schoole der Schilderkunst*, Rotterdam 1678, from the original edition (p. 312).
The painting in New York, now exhibited as a work of Hercules Seghers, was first mentioned in the context of Seghers' work by Wolfgang Stechow, *Salomon van Ruysdael, eine Einführung in seine Kunst*, Berlin 1838, p. 58, and attributed to the artist in 1958 by this writer among the 'theses' accompanying his doctoral dissertation, Utrecht University.

Biographical Data

1589/90 Born, son of Pieter Segers and Cathalyntgen Hercules, probably in Haarlem.

Until December 1606 In Amsterdam, pupil of Gillis van Coninxloo.

March 1–6 1607 At the public sale of the estate of Gillis van Coninxloo, Hercules Seghers buys *Een steenrootsken van Coninxloo met vergulden lijst* ('A small rocky landscape by Coninxloo in a guilded frame').

December 19 1614 Settlement with the mother of a child of his born out of wedlock.

December 27 1614 Posting of the banns of *Hercules Pietersz van Haerlem, Schilder, 24 jaer a puero N.Z. Achterburgwal* ('Hercules Pietersz of Haarlem, Painter, 24 years old, N.Z.A. [Amsterdam]').

January 10 1615 At Sloterdijk, *herkeles pieters* contracts marriage with Anneken van der Brugghen.

July 17 1618 *Hercules Pieters schilder* and his wife file a last will and testament.

May 14 1619 *Hercules Pietersz* buys a house called *daer de Hartoch van Gelder in de Gevel staet* situated on the Lindengracht in Amsterdam from Thomas Jacobsz Haringh (later portrayed by Rembrandt), and occupies this.

1621 A painting by *Hercules Pietersen* is offered by Theodoor Rodenburg to Christian IV, King of Denmark.

June 21 1621 For the first time named *Hercules Segers.*

1623, 1626 Mentioned as living in Amsterdam.

1627 Two paintings by Seghers listed in the estate of the Amsterdam painter Louys Rocourt; one landscape painting in the estate of the Rotterdam artist Herman Saftleven.

1629 Mentioned as living in Amsterdam.

January 4 1631 The house in Amsterdam on the Lindengracht publicly sold for execution of debts.

May 21 1631 Hercules Seghers, *Schilder, residerende tot Utrecht in the Wittevrouwenstraat,* sells paintings.

1632 *Twee lantschappen deur Hercules Zegers gemaekt* are listed in the collections of the House of Orange.

January 28 1633 *hercules segers* mentioned as *jegenwoordich wonende alhier in den Hage* ('at present living here in The Hague').

February 13 1633 A legal document mentions a house in The Hague *daer Hercules de Haerlem in 1632 metter woone was gecomen* ('of which Hercules of Haarlem had taken occupancy in 1632').

1638 Cornelia de Witte is mentioned in The Hague as widow of *Hercules Pietersz* (= Hercules Seghers?).

IV

11

13

14

15

abbey at Byurs bury

16

17

19